QUICK STUDY® ACADEMIC — AMERICAN HIST

D0864215

THE NEW WORLD 1492-1646

- **1492** **Christopher Columbus** lands in the Bahamas.
- **1513** **Ponce de Leon** lands in Florida.
- **1518** **Smallpox**, brought by the Europeans, begins to decimate the native population of Central and South America. The epidemic will last until 1530.
- **1521** Aztec chief Tenochtitlan surrenders to Spanish explorer/conqueror **Ferdinand Cortes**, and his empire falls.
- **1533** **Henry VIII** starts the English Reformation mainly to gain a divorce from Catherine of Aragon.
- **1539** **Hernando de Soto** begins exploration of what will be the southeastern United States.
- **1540** **Francisco Vasquez de Coronado** does the same in the southwest.
- **1558** Henry VIII's daughter **Elizabeth I** becomes Queen of England.
- **1587** **1587-90: Sir Walter Raleigh** starts, and fails, with a colony in **Roanoke** (an island off North Carolina); the first attempt in North America.
- **1588** The English navy, helped by violent storms, defeats the Spanish Armada.
- **1603** **James I** becomes King of England.
- **1603** **1603-05: Samuel de Champlain** of France explores what will be present day Canada.
- **1607** Jamestown (Virginia) is founded.
- **1611** The first Virginia tobacco crop is harvested.
- **1619** The first African-Americans arrive in Virginia.
- **1620** Plymouth Colony (Massachusetts) is founded.
- **1622** The Powhatan Confederacy attacks the Virginia Colony.
- **1624** The Dutch settle Manhattan Island.
- **1625** **Charles I** becomes King of England.
- **1630** The Massachusetts Bay Colony is founded.
- **1634** Maryland is founded as a "haven for English Catholics."
- **1635** **Roger Williams** is "expelled" from The Massachusetts Bay Colony, and founds Providence (Rhode Island).
- **1636** Connecticut is founded.
- **1637** 1. The Pequot War virtually wipes out the Pequot Indian tribe.
  2. **Anne Marbury Hutchinson** and her followers are exiled to Rhode Island, from Massachusetts Bay Colony, for preaching what the Puritan elite call heresy.
- **1646** **Virginia and the Powhatan Confederacy** sign a peace treaty.

A SOCIETY FORMS 1642-1732

- **1642** **1642-46: The English Civil War** sends many in search of the "New World."
- **1649** **King Charles I** is executed.
- **1660** 1. The **House of Stuart** returns to the throne of England, and King Charles II rules.
- **1662** The **"Halfway Covenant"** is drafted in Massachusetts:
  a. Adults who had been baptized but were not full church members could have their children baptized if they recognized Church authority and lived by its precepts.
  b. They could not, however, vote or take communion.
- **1663** Carolina is chartered.
- **1664** England defeats the Dutch and takes over New Amsterdam, naming it New York.
- **1675** **"King Philip's War"**
  a. Chief Metacomet ("King Philip") of Pokanet tribe rises against Pilgrim encroachment of tribal lands.
  b. Destroys 12 of 90 Puritan towns.
  c. Lack of food and ammunition brings about defeat.
  d. Metacomet killed. Tribe virtually wiped out except in Martha's Vineyard area.
- **1676** **Bacon's Rebellion** in Virginia
  a. Farmer **Nathaniel Bacon** rouses farmers to fight Indians.
  b. **Governor William Berkeley** declares him "in rebellion."
  c. Bacon marches on Jamestown and burns capitol to the ground. When he dies of dysentery, the rebellion collapses.
  1. **Pueblo Revolt**
- **1680** a. Led by Medicine Man **Pope (po-pay)**, Pueblos in New Mexico revolt against Spaniards and drive them out.
  b. Spaniards out of power until 1692, when they engender new spirit of cooperation with Indians.
  2. Maryland colonists, "forced" to eat the oysters along their shore to keep from starvation, found a new industry.

A COUNTRY GROWS 1690-1771

- **1690** John Locke writes an *Essay Concerning Human Rights*, a major contribution to the era known as "The Enlightenment."
- **1691** The **Massachusetts Colony** gets a new charter giving it all North American Territories north to the St. Lawrence River.
- **1693** The **College of William and Mary** is founded in the Virginia Colony.
- **1695** The city of **Annapolis** is laid out in Maryland to serve as the colonial capitol.
- **1701** The city of **Detroit** is founded as the French settlement Fort Pontchatrain on a strait between Lake Erie and Lake St. Clair.
- **1720** **Smallpox** epidemic hits Boston.
  a. Cotton Mather urges citizens to try new technique called **"inoculation."**
  b. Those that get inoculated survive in five times greater numbers.
- **1720** **1720-40:** The Black population of Chesapeake grows substantially through natural increase.
- **1739** 1. Slaves in the **Stono River** area of South Carolina arm themselves and rebel.
  a. Head for Florida hoping for refuge in the Spanish Colony.
  b. Militia puts down rebellion in a day.
  c. All blacks involved are killed immediately or executed subsequently.
  2. **"King George's War"** begins with Spain.
  a. Combined with Stono Rebellion, this feeds fears of whites against Black uprising and leads to a reign of terror in New York against imagined "conspirators."
  b. War will end in 1748.
  3. George Whitefield arrives in America and spreads the teachings of **"The Great Awakening."**
- **1765** The **Hudson River Land Riots** of squatters against powerful landowners lead to almost a year long control of the Hudson River valley by insurgents.
- **1767** **"Regulator"** movement starts in South Carolina.
  a. Essentially a "vigilante" movement against perceived lax law enforcement.
  b. Will spawn a "regulator" movement in North Carolina.
- **1769** **South Carolina Regulator** movement ends.
- **1770** 21 year-old Boston printer **Isaiah Thomas** begins publication of *The Massachusetts Spy,* one of the earliest pro-colonist/anti-British newspapers.
- **1771** North Carolina movement ends in fierce battle between regulators and militia at the **Battle of Alamance.**

- **1681** **Pennsylvania** is chartered.
- **1682** **James II** is King of England.
- **1686** Dominion of New England is formed.
  a. Charters of all individual states revoked due to "Non English" practices.
  b. **Sir Edmund Andros** is named Governor of Dominion.
- **1688** **James II** is deposed in the "Glorious Revolution." **William & Mary** gain the throne.
- **1689** 1. Dominion of New England is overthrown.
  a. Andros jailed.
  b. Return to former state charters hoped for but not achieved.
  2. **"King William's War"**
  a. A.k.a. The War of the League of Augsburg.
  b. Americans fight on Northern Frontiers.
  c. Many colonies are decimated.
  d. Ends in 1697.
- **1692** **Salem Witchcraft** hysteria
  a. Brought on by tensions from "King William's War."
  b. Started as a "prank" by a group of adolescent girls.
  c. Nineteen people executed. Hundreds imprisoned.
  d. For further information, see: *The Crucible* by Arthur Miller.
- **1696** **The Board of Trade and Plantations**, the chief organ of British Government in respect to the American Colonies, is established.
- **1701** **Iroquois Nation** adopts policy of neutrality.
- **1702** **"Queen Anne's War"** begins.
  a. AKA: The War of the Spanish Succession.
  b. Although bearing a heavy economic burden on colonies, has less effect than "King William's War."
  c. Will end in 1713.
- **1711** **Tuscarora War** begins in North Carolina.
  a. Tuscarora Indians were trading members of other tribes as slaves.
  b. These tribes joined English to fight against them.
- **1713** Tuscarora War ends.
- **1715** **Yamasee War** in South Carolina is a protest against English mistreatment and slavery.
- **1732** **Georgia** is chartered.

REVOLUTIONARY IDEAS 1754-1774

- **1754** 1. **Albany Congress** is convened by delegates from seven British northern and middle colonies in response to French activities on the western frontiers.
  a. It attempts to convince Iroquois to abandon neutrality and join English, and to coordinate colonial defenses.
  b. Both goals fail.
  2. **French and Indian War** begins.
- **1760** 1. British dismissal of abilities of colonial soldiers in the French-Indian war leads to a furthering of dissension between colonies and home country.
  2. **George III** becomes King of England.
- **1763** 1. **Treaty of Paris** is signed. France cedes all major North American holdings to England. Spain cedes Florida.
  2. **Pontiac**, war chief of an Ottowa village near Detroit, unites tribes and lays siege to a Detroit fort while his troops attack other British outposts in the region a protest against encroaching British rule.
  3. **Proclamation Of 1763** in effect "apologizes" to the Indians for encroachment and declares a strict, temporary, boundary for colonial settlement.
- **1764** **Sugar Act**, designed specifically to enrich England, raises new duties on imports to the New World, infuriating the colonists.
- **1765** **Stamp Act** imposes a heavy tax on colonies.
  a. The **"Sons of Liberty"** are formed to unite colonials in opposition to the taxes. Some of the protests get violent.
- **1766** Stamp Act is repealed, but **Declaratory Act** asserts Britain's ability to tax and legislate for American possessions "in all cases whatsoever."
- **1767** **Townshend Acts** impose larger taxes on colonials.
- **1770** 1. Lord North becomes Prime Minister of Britain.
  2. Townshend Acts are repealed... except the tax on tea.
  3. **Boston Massacre** lights the fuse on American resentment at its highest.
- **1772** **Boston Committee of Correspondence** is formed and urges an immediate boycott of all British goods.
- **1773** **Tea Act** eliminates colonial middlemen, and profits to them, from tea trade. Colonial reaction leads directly to **Boston Tea Party.**
- **1774** **Coercive Acts**, better known as "Intolerable Acts," are implemented by Lord North, fanning the fuse for revolution.

THE REVOLUTION 1774-1783

- **1774** **First Continental Congress** is convened.
- **1775** 1. **Lord Dunmore's** proclamation is issued. In a letter to General Thomas Gage, Dunmore downplays any chance of significant revolution from "rude rabble without a plan."
  2. **Battles of Lexington and Concord** are fought; **Revolutionary War** officially begins.
  3. **Second Continental Congress** is convened. Originally intended as "interim," it becomes, in essence, the country's Seat of Government.
- **1776** 1. Thomas Paine writes *Common Sense,* rallying Americans.
  2. The British evacuate Boston.
  3. **Thomas Jefferson** writes, and the Congress signs, **The Declaration of Independence.** Anti-slavery clauses omitted due to Southern pressure.
  4. **Battle for New York City** is fought.
  a. **General George Washington** proves a formidable foe.
  b. Delays on British side add to America's strength.
- **1777** 1. The British capture Philadelphia.
  2. British General **Burgoyne** surrenders at Saratoga (New York).
- **1778** 1. France joins the battle on America's side.
  2. The British evacuate Philadelphia.
- **1779** **General John Sullivan** leads an expedition against the Iroquois for their support of British forces, which destroy all crops, orchards, and settlements.
- **1780** British control Charleston (South Carolina).
- **1781** **General Cornwallis surrenders** at Yorktown.
- **1782** Peace negotiations begin in Paris.
- **1783** **Treaty of Paris** gives America unconditional independence and establishes America's boundaries, while ignoring territorial claims of Native Americans.

A NATION IS FORMED 1776-1800

1776
1. **Second Continental Congress** directs each state to draft an individual constitution.
2. North Carolina extends its jurisdiction by annexing the Watagua settlement, now calling it Washington County.

1777
1. **Articles of Confederation** forming the "united" states are sent to the states for ratification.
2. New Connecticut "republic" renames itself Vermont, and adopts a constitution mandating suffrage for all men and banning slavery.

1778
Sandwich Islands, later to become the state of Hawaii, are discovered by **Captain James Cook**.

1779
The first written report on the planting and use of sweet corn (discovered along the Susquehanna River) is published.

1780
To control rampant inflation, Congress passes the **"40 to 1" Act**, stating that continental paper money will be redeemed at one-fortieth of its face value. The phrase "...not worth a continental" enters common speech.

1781
Articles of Confederation are ratified.

1782
Congress adopts the Great Seal of the United States.

1783
1. Virginia House of Burgesses grants freedom to any black slaves who served in the Continental Army.
2. George Washington issues his **"Farewell Address to the Army,"** and all troops are formally discharged.
3. **Noah Webster** publishes *Webster's Spelling Book*, codifying American words and spelling for the first time.
   a. First of a 3 book cycle entitled *A Grammatical Institute of the English Language, Comprising an Easy, Concise and Systematic Method of Education, Designed for the Use of English Schools in America*.
   b. In 1828 he will publish *An American Dictionary of the English Language*.

1784
The British transport all **Acadians** to Maine and Louisiana where, combining their Canadian origins with the "injun" style of life and cookery, they become known as **"Cajun."**

1785
Congress establishes the **dollar** as the **official U.S. currency** using a decimal system devised by Thomas Jefferson.

1786
Annapolis (Maryland) **Convention** is held to discuss U.S. trade policies.
   a. Eight states name representatives but only five attend.
   b. Another convention called for in Philadelphia in nine months.

1786
Farmer **Daniel Shays** leads a rebellion against high taxes and low money supply in western Massachusetts. Because Shays and many others involved are "gentlemen" (i.e. landowners), government is forced to rethink policies.

1787
1. **Northwest Ordinance** guarantees settlers in the Northwest Territories many of the freedoms later to be incorporated into The Bill of Rights.
2. **Constitutional Convention** convenes.
   a. The Constitution of the United States is signed on September 17.
   b. Benjamin Franklin states: "...there are several parts of the constitution which I do not...approve (but) I expect no better and I am not sure that it is not the best."

1788
1. James Madison, John Jay, and Alexander Hamilton urge New York's (and the nation's) ratification of the Constitution in the publication *The Federalist*, which explains the meaning of the Constitution and assures immediate addition of **Bill Of Rights**.
2. The Constitution is ratified.

1789
United States House of Representatives holds its first meeting on April 1; 30 days before George Washington assumes the office of president.

1790
The first successful U.S. cotton mill is established in what will become Pawtucket, Rhode Island.

1791
Bill of Rights becomes U.S. law with Virginia's ratification.

1792
Eli Whitney invents the cotton gin.

1793
President Washington meets, at his home, with the heads of his departments of State, Treasury, and War, the Attorney General and the Postmaster General, thereby holding **the first "cabinet" meeting**.

1794
Battle of Fallen Timbers (Ohio), led by General "Mad" Anthony Wayne, defeats Indian tribes demanding territorial rights and opens way for negotiations on settlement of the area.

1795
Treaty of Greenville signed by Wayne and delegates from the Miami (Indian) Confederacy gives U.S. right to settle the Ohio Territory.

1799
Charles Brockden Brown publishes *Arthur Mervyn*, the first novel to use distinctly American characters and settings.

1800
Parson Mason Locke Weems publishes his *Life of Washington*.
   a. Any resemblance to the actual life of the President is purely accidental.
   b. The "cherry tree" fable.

THE EARLY REPUBLIC 1789-1800

1789
1. **George Washington** is inaugurated as the first president.
2. **Judiciary Act** provides for a **Supreme Court** of six members, including a Chief Justice and five associate justices.
   a. Defines jurisdiction of the federal judiciary.
   b. Establishes 13 district courts and 3 circuit courts of appeal.
3. **French Revolution** begins.
4. Congress passes the **first Tariff Act.**
5. 12 Amendments are proposed to the Constitution.
6. **Georgetown University** has its beginnings.
7. The first American advertisement for tobacco appears.
8. Baptist Minister **Elijah Craig** distills the first bourbon whiskey in the Kentucky region.
9. Nine out of ten Americans are engaged in farming and food production.

1790
1. Secretary of the Treasury **Alexander Hamilton** issues the first **Report on Public Credit**, aiming to expand financial reach of federal government and reduce power of the states.
2. The House of Representatives votes to locate the nation's capital on a 10-mile stretch along the Potomac River.
3. Congress establishes the first U.S. Patent Office.

1791
1. The **Bill of Rights** is ratified.
2. Vermont becomes the 14th state to enter the union.

1792
Thomas Paine publishes *The Rights of Man*, arguing that power should rest with the democratic majority.

1793
1. France declares war on Britain, Spain, and Holland. U.S. remains neutral.
2. Democratic-Republican Societies, sympathetic to French cause, are founded.
3. **Thomas Jefferson** resigns as Secretary of State to head the anti-federalist Democratic-Republican Party.
4. Congress passes the **Fugitive Slave Act**.

1794
1. The **Whiskey Rebellion** against high taxes leads Washington to send troops to Pennsylvania to avoid repeat of **Shays Rebellion**.
2. America's first trade union, The **Federal Society of Journeymen Cordwainers** (shoemakers), is organized.
3. General "Mad" Anthony Wayne wins the **Battle of Fallen Timbers** ending the Indian "threat" to settlers in the Ohio-Kentucky region.

1795
1. The **Jay Treaty** resolves issues of Anglo-American affairs, averting war.
2. **First railroad** in America, a wooden railed tramway running the slope of Beacon Hill, is built in Boston.

1796
1. The first contested presidential election is held. John Adams (Federalist Party) is elected. **Thomas Jefferson** (Republican) is vice president.
2. The Supreme Court rules on the constitutionality of an act of Congress for the first time, *Hylton v United States*.

1797
First ship of the **United States Navy**, called, appropriately, the *United States*, is launched.

1798
1. The **"XYZ Affair"** shows France treating America with disdain and leads to wave of anti-French sentiment.
2. **Alien and Sedition Acts**, four laws designed by Federalists to prevent dissent and the growth of Republican Party, are passed.
3. **Virginia and Kentucky Resolutions** repudiate the Alien and Sedition Acts.
4. Congress establishes the **Marine Hospital Service**, which will later become the U.S. Public Health Service.
5. Eli Whitney pioneers the "American System" of **mass production** to build firearms.
6. The first professional American writer, Charles Brockden Brown, publishes *Alcuin: A Dialogue on the Rights of Women*.

1799
1. U.S. and France engage in undeclared war in the West Indies a.k.a. "The Quasi-War."
2. **George Washington dies**.
   a. General Henry ("Lighthorse Harry") Lee delivers a eulogy declaring Washington "First in War, first in peace, and first in the hearts of his countrymen."

1800
1. **Franco-American Convention** ends the Quasi-War and frees U.S. from obligations to France from the **Treaty of 1778**.
2. **Thomas Jefferson** is elected president. **Aaron Burr** is vice president.
3. The Second Great Awakening, a wave of revivalism, provides religious fervor and revolutionary zeal to many women.
4. **Gabriel's Rebellion**, a black revolt in Virginia led by Gabriel Prosser, where the participants demand equal rights.
5. Congress passes the **Public Land Act**, a.k.a. the **Harrison Land Act**, providing liberal credit terms for land purchase and encouraging speculation in real estate and expansion.

LIBERTY GROWS 1801-1823

1801
1. **Thomas Jefferson** is inaugurated.
2. **John Marshall** named Chief Justice of the Supreme Court.
3. Jefferson refuses to pay tribute to the Sultan of Tripoli (Africa) to protect U.S. ships from Barbary Pirates. Sends naval squadron to the Mediterranean instead.

1803
1. Navy begins **blockade of Tripoli Harbor**.
2. *Marbury v Madison* establishes the Supreme Court's power to judge constitutionality of issues.
3. **Louisiana Purchase**, 877,000 square miles, expands U.S. territories westward, doubling the size of the country.

1804
1. Marines march into the port of Derna (Tripoli).
2. Thomas Jefferson is re-elected.
3. **Lewis and Clark** expedition begins.

1805
Peace treaty signed in Tripoli.

1806
Lewis and Clark expedition ends with information on vast territories in the northwest.

1807
1. *Chesapeake Affair* exposes U.S. military weakness, as British ship destroys U.S. ship *Chesapeake* within U.S. territorial waters.
2. **Embargo Act** forbids all U.S. exports and virtually eliminates imports.

1808
James Madison is elected president.

1812
War of 1812 begins with the British.

1814
1. **Treaty of Ghent** on Christmas Eve halts hostilities.
2. **Hartford Convention** sees conservative Republicans attempting to limit the powers of the President and radically change the Constitution.

1815
Andrew Jackson becomes a hero at **Battle of New Orleans**. Fought *after* the war had officially ended (unbeknownst to Jackson).

1816
1. **James Monroe** is elected president.
2. Second Bank of the United States is chartered.

1817
Rush-Bagot Treaty leads to the demilitarization of the U.S./Canadian border.

1819
1. In *McCulloch v Maryland*, Chief Justice John Marshall establishes that the Supreme Court supercedes state courts in matters of Federal rights.
2. **Adams-Onis Treaty** cedes Florida to the U.S. and sets U.S. southern border.

1820
1. **Missouri Compromise** prohibits slavery in Louisiana Territory states north of Missouri's southern boundary.
2. Monroe is re-elected.

1823
Monroe Doctrine declares "most of the Western Hemisphere" off limits to foreign (European) intervention.

LOOKING AT LIFE 1655-1806

1655
Lady **Deborah Moody**, in a Long Island (New York) Town Meeting, is the first woman allowed to vote.

1662
Michael Wigglesworth publishes *Day of Doom, or a poetical description of the Great and Last Judgement*, a bestseller, on the torments of hell awaiting sinners.

1673
First mail service is established between Boston and New York.

1700
First publicly supported library is established in Charleston.

1701
Six women sit on a jury in Albany, N.Y., denoting growing respect for women in public life.

1704
The first regularly published newspaper, *Boston NewsLetter*, is published by John Campbell.

1714
Tea is introduced to the colonies.

1723
Old North Church is built.

1729
Ben Franklin begins publishing what will become *The Saturday Evening Post*.

1734
John Peter Zenger is imprisoned for 10 months because of "seditious libels" (i.e. stories not to the liking of the established authority) in his newspaper.

1735
Zenger's paper endorses the Popular Party candidates for alderman; they win.

1737
The first celebration of St. Patrick's Day is held in Boston.

1743
Ben Franklin retires from business at the age of 37.

1789
1. **Society of Saint Tammany** is established in New York. It will become the epitome of power politics in the U.S.
2. First national **Thanksgiving Day** is established.

1790
Dobson's Encyclopedia, an American version of the *Encyclopedia Britannica*, is published.

1793
The cornerstone is laid for the new Capitol Building on the Potomac River.

1800
Congress authorizes franking privileges (free postage) for Martha Washington and for Revolutionary war vets.

1806
Washington Irving publishes his first stories and establishes the Knickerbocker School of Authentically American Writing.

LIFE GOES ON 1807-1857

1807 **Robert Fulton** presents the first steamboat, the *Clermont*.

1813 **Boston Manufacturing Company** is founded.
  a. Uses the first American power loom, which radically changes textile manufacturing.
  b. Combines all manufacturing processes under one roof.

1818 National Road, a stone-based, gravel top highway beginning in Cumberland, Maryland, reaches Wheeling, W. Virginia. It will reach Columbus, Ohio by 1833.

1819 *Dartmouth College v Woodward* establishes non-interference by states in commerce and business where a "contract" exists.

1820 **1820 and beyond** New England textile mills expand and dominate the market.

1824 *Gibbons v Ogden*: Supreme Court ends monopoly on steamboat trade by ruling that Congress, not individual states, controls commerce as per the "commerce clause" of the Constitution.

1825 **Erie Canal** is completed.

1830 **Baltimore & Ohio Railroad** starts operating.

1831 Cyrus McCormick invents the **McCormick Reaper**, vastly improving farm productivity and efficiency.

1834 Due to "unfair practices" at the Lowell (Mass.) textile mills, the mill workers, all women, "Turn Out" (i.e. go on strike). The strike is unsuccessful and leads to even greater pressures on workers.

1837 *Charles River Bridge v Warren Bridge* establishes that new enterprises cannot be restricted by implied privileges under old charters which they were not party to.

1839 An economic depression begins, lasting until 1843.

1844 Baltimore-Washington telegraph line is established.

1848 The discovery of gold at Sutter's Mill (California) starts the great **California "Gold Rush."**

1853 The British begin a study of the American manufacturing system.

1854 The railroad reaches the Mississippi.

1857 A new depression begins.

AMERICAN GROWTH 1805-1849

1805 Shawnee Indian Chiefs **Prophet and Tecumseh** emerge as leaders preaching a united front against U.S. encroachment and military might. They will align with British in War of 1812.

10 New York City surpasses Philadelphia in population.

1813 **Tecumseh** dies, as does hope of a united front against U.S. treaty policies.

1819 **Indian Civilization Act** is passed, aimed at assimilating tribes into the white mainstream through government financial aid and boarding schools.

1823 **Catherine and Mary Beecher** establish the Hartford Female Seminary to teach young women to be teachers.
  a. Seen as an extension of women's "nurturing" role in society.
  b. Will establish teaching as *the* role for educated women in the workplace.

1824 President James Monroe proposes removal of all Indians to lands west of the Mississippi, an "honorable" move to assure Indian's right to dwell in peace.

1827 *Freedom's Journal*, the first Black weekly, begins publication.

1831 *Cherokee Nation v Georgia* attempts to fight Monroe's removal policy through legal means.
  a. Chief Justice John Marshall rules that Indians are neither a foreign nation nor a state, and so have no standing in a federal court.

1831 **Trail of Tears** begins when the Choctaw (Miss. & Ala.) tribe is forced to lands west of the Mississippi.

1832 Justice John Marshall clarifies his position regarding the Cherokee by stating that the Indian Nation is a distinct political community in which the "laws of the state of Georgia can have no force."
  a. Further, forbids Georgians from entering without permission or treaty privilege.
  b. This is ignored and the Trail of Tears continues.

1835 **Seminole War** erupts. Led by Osceola, the Seminoles will battle until 1842.

1837 The city of Boston employs paid policemen.

1845 A potato famine starts in Ireland, leading to mass Irish immigration -- 1.3 million by 1857.

1848 An abortive revolution in Germany is the impetus for German immigration -- 1.1 million by 1857.

1849 A theater riot erupts in New York:
  a. As theaters were the place where people of all classes and races mixed in the same building, they became the arenas for "class wars."
  b. This riot is culmination of many smaller ones starting as early as 1830.

EXPANSION & REFORM 1825-1848

1825
1. The House of Representatives elects **John Quincy Adams** president.
2. Adams delivers the first presidential message to Congress, urging growth, reform, establishment of a national university system, and an astronomical observatory in Washington.
3. 600 Boston carpenters go on strike arguing for a 10-hour workday in U.S.
4. Fur trader Pierre Cabanne opens a **trading post** on the Missouri River, which will become **Omaha** (Nebraska).
5. **General Simon Perkins founds Akron (Ohio)**.

1826
1. American Society for the Promotion of Temperance is founded to defeat **"demon rum."**
2. Anti-Masonry becomes an organized movement when disillusioned Mason William Morgan, writes "expose" *The Illustration of Masonry by One of the Fraternity Who Has Devoted Thirty Years to the Subject*.
3. The first overland journey to Southern California leaves Great Salt Lake on August 22, arrives in San Diego on November 27.
4. Gideon B. Smith plants first Chinese mulberry trees in U.S., giving impetus to silk trade.
5. **Lyceum movement** led by Josiah Holbrook spreads interest in the arts, sciences, and "public issues" throughout the eastern U.S.

1827 Creek Indians cede their western Georgia lands to the U.S.

1828
1. Passage of **Tariff of Abominations** leads southern states to devise the Doctrine of Nullification, giving states the right to overrule federal legislation in conflict with their own.
2. **Andrew Jackson** is elected president.
3. Construction begins on Baltimore and Ohio railroad.
4. **Delaware and Hudson Canal** opens, linking Kingston, N.Y. with Port Jervis, where it connects with the Lackawanna Canal to Honesdale, PA., a distance of 108 miles.

1829 **American Society for Encouraging Settlement in Oregon** is established in Boston after Congress defeats a bill to set up a territorial government there.

1830
1. The (Daniel) **Webster-** (Robert Y.) **Hayne Debates** discuss the notion of nullification and the meaning of "union."
2. A second (political) party system begins to develop.

1831
1. *Liberator*, an anti-slavery journal, begins publication.
2. The first national Anti-Mason Convention is held.

1832
1. **Andrew Jackson** vetoes rechartering of the Second Bank of the United States.
2. Jackson re-elected president.

1833 Americans living in **Texas** vote to separate from Mexico.

1834 The U.S. government demands Seminoles leave Florida as per an 1832 treaty.

1835 Mexico proclaims a unified constitution that abolishes slavery. U.S. citizens living in Texas vote to secede rather than give up this right.

1836
1. **Republic of Texas** is established.
2. To end public land monopoly of speculators and capitalists, the **Specie Circular** states that only specie (gold or silver) or Virginia land scrip is acceptable payment for land.
3. **Martin Van Buren** is elected president.

1837
1. A financial panic hits the U.S.
2. Tensions rise along the U.S./Canada border.
3. **Horace Mann** is named first head of the Massachusetts Board of Education, a position he will hold until 1848.

1838 **Underground Railroad** is organized by abolitionists to provide slaves an escape route to the North.

1839 U.S. enters a **depression** that will last until 1843.

1840 **William Henry Harrison** (Whig Party) wins presidency.

1841
1. **Brook Farm**, a cooperative that rejects materialism and seeks satisfaction in communal life, founded by Unitarian Minister George Ripley.
2. Upon Harrison's death (after less than a month in office) **John Tyler** becomes president.
3. Missionaries report the "wonders" of the Oregon Territory leading to **"Oregon Fever"** for expansion.

1843 European support for an independent Texas causes U.S. interest.

1844 **James Polk** is elected president.

1845 Texas joins the union.

1847
1. **Mormons** arrive in Utah Territory.
2. First Chinese immigrants arrive in New York.

1848
1. **Women's Rights Convention** is held in Seneca Falls, N.Y.
2. New York becomes base for the **Cunard Steamship Line**, making it the center of European travel to and from the New World.
3. A telegraph line opens from New York to Chicago.
4. The **Oneida Community**, the first communal society in the U.S., is formed in central New York.
5. Pennsylvania enacts a child labor law restricting worker's age.

SLAVERY 1712-1865

1712
1. A **Black Insurrection** is staged in New York; 21 blacks are executed.
2. Pennsylvania Colony enacts legislation banning the importation of slaves.

1713 England's **South Sea Company** is granted permission to import 4800 slaves per year into the Spanish colonies of North America for a period of 30 years.

1716 **First black slaves** arrive in French territory of Louisiana.

1724 French Louisiana Governor de Bienville establishes a code to regulate behavior of Blacks.

1725
1. Slave population is estimated at 75,000.
2. Right to a separate black Baptist Church granted in Williamsburg, (Virginia).

1731 An English order prohibits implementing duty on imported slaves by the colonial legislatures.

1735 Colonist John Van Zandt (New York) horsewhips his slave so severely the slave dies, and a coroner's jury attributes the death to a "visitation of God."

1739 Three separate **black insurrections** occur in South Carolina.

1740 A planned revolt by Charleston (S.C.) slaves revealed; 50 slaves hanged.

1741 **New York City panic** based on (unfounded) fears of a black uprising leads to 18 Blacks hanged, 13 Blacks burned to death, and 70 banished.

1743 New Jersey **Clergyman John Woolman** preaches against slavery.

1749 **Georgia Colony** revokes a prohibition against slavery, giving it legal recognition and starting the plantation system.

1772 In the *Sommersett Case*, Chief Justice Lord Mansfield declares a slave free the moment he sets foot on English soil.

1773 Yale President Ezra Stiles and Clergyman Samuel Hopkins propose colonizing West Africa with freed slaves.

1775 Benjamin Franklin and Dr. Benjamin Rush establish the **Society for the Relief of Free Negroes Unlawfully Held in Bondage**.

1780 The Pennsylvania legislature mandates the gradual abolition of slavery within the State.

1788 The Massachusetts legislature enacts a bill making slave trade illegal.

1790 The **Society of Friends** (Quakers) presents the first petition calling for the abolition of slavery to Congress.

1791 **Slave uprising in Haiti** leads to slave revolt in Spanish Louisiana.

1792
1. **Clergyman David Rice** fails in his attempt to get the Kentucky constitutional convention to outlaw slavery.
2. Virginia Statesman George Mason leads his state's opposition to slavery.

1793 Congress enacts the **Fugitive Slave Act**.

1794 Congress bans slave trade with foreign nations.

1799 New York passes a gradual emancipation law.

1800 "Gabriel's Rebellion" (q.v.)

1808 Congress passes legislation forbidding foreign slave trade.

1816 Clergyman Robert Finley founds **The American Colonization Society** to resettle freed slaves in Africa. Establishes the Republic of Liberia.

1820
1. **Missouri Compromise**
2. Congress makes trade in foreign slaves an "act of piracy."

1821 Benjamin Lundy publishes *The Genius of Universal Emancipation*, one of the earliest abolition journals.

1822 A planned slave revolt in Charleston, South Carolina by freed black **Denmark Vesey** is thwarted.

1830 A schooner out of Virginia, bound for New Orleans, is wrecked off the Bahamas. British authorities declare the slaves it was carrying free.

1832 The **Virginia Assembly debates abolition**.

1836 The **Massachusetts Supreme Court** frees any slave brought across the state border.

1837 Frederick Douglas escapes to freedom and becomes 1st "fugitive slave" lecturer speaking in America and abroad and leading equal rights demonstrations.

1841 The **Supreme Court** rules that 53 black mutineers from the Spanish slave ship Amistad, who had been taken into U.S. custody, shall be free to return to Africa.

1845 *Narrative of the Life of Frederick Douglas* is published, followed by establishment of the newspaper *North Star*.

1850 Practice of selling slaves to new, and less "comfortable" plantations further south along the Mississippi causes **"sold down the river"** to enter language.

1859
1. Georgia passes a law banning wills or deeds granting freedom to slaves, and enacts legislation allowing any black indicted for vagrancy to be sold.
2. President James Buchanan opposes slave trade, yet bans searches of U.S. ships by British patrols thus giving virtual immunity to continue the trade.

1861 **Civil War** begins.
1. Northern states have a population of over 22 million.
2. The Confederacy has 10 million, of which over one third are slaves.

1862 Congress abolishes slavery in District of Columbia and U.S. Territories.

1863 **Emancipation Proclamation** frees slaves *only* in those states at war against the Union.

1865 **Civil War** ends. **Thirteenth Amendment**, freeing slaves in both North and South, is ratified.

THE ROAD WEST - TO WAR 1846-1861

1846
1. **War with Mexico** begins over Texas borders and lands west that President James Polk wants for U.S.
2. Representative **David Wilmot** (D. Penn.) offers an amendment to a war appropriations bill: *"...neither slavery nor involuntary servitude shall ever exist..."* in territories won from Mexico. It fails but becomes the rallying cry for "Free Soilers" and abolitionists.

1847 Presidential nominee **General Lewis Cass** (D.) proposes **Popular Sovereignty** (each territory to decide whether to be "slave" or "free").

1848 **Zachary Taylor** is elected President.

1849 California applies for admission to the U.S.

1850 **Compromise of 1850**, devised by Senators **Henry** ("The Great Pacificator") **Clay** and **Stephen A.** ("The Little Giant") **Douglas**, admits California as a free state, gives New Mexico and Utah territories power to legislate *"all rightful subjects...consistent with the Constitution"* (i.e. slavery) and promises stronger fugitive slave laws and suppression of slave trade in the **District of Columbia**.

1852
1. **Harriet Beecher Stowe's** *Uncle Tom's Cabin* is published and influences anti-slavery feelings. **Abraham Lincoln** will call Stowe "The little lady who started the war."
2. **Franklin Pierce** is elected President.

1854
1. **Kansas-Nebraska Act** repeals slavery limitations set by the Missouri Compromise, allowing Kansas and Nebraska territories to be slave owning if they so choose. In the *Appeal of the Independent Democrats,* six congressman call this *"a gross violation of a sacred pledge."*
2. **Republican Party** is formed and makes inroads against the Democrats in congressional elections.

1856
1. Battles over slavery in **Kansas** earn it the nickname "Bleeding Kansas."
2. Senator **Charles Sumner** of Massachusetts denounces the *"crime against Kansas,"* and is brutally beaten on the Senate floor by Representative **Preston Brooks** of South Carolina.
3. **James Buchanan** is elected President.

1857
1. *Dred Scott v Sanford* effectively voids the Missouri Compromise.
   a. Scott, a Missouri slave, had sued for freedom, stating that he had been taken so frequently into free territory that he was a resident there.
   b. Supreme Court rules Scott *"not a citizen"*; therefore not free; and, in any event, Congress could not bar slavery from a territory.
2. **Lecompton Constitution** (Kansas), permits slavery. It is defeated in 1858 after anti-slavery forces are elected to the majority.

1858
1. Presidential nominee **Stephen A. Douglas** (D) begins a series of cross-country debates with nominee **Abraham Lincoln** (R).
   a. Douglas' **Freeport Doctrine** states that territorial legislatures can bar slavery either by passing such a law or not enforcing slavery laws.
2. A composer identified only as **"JK"** writes *The Yellow Rose of Texas.*
3. **Iowa State College** and **Oregon State University** are founded.

1859 Abolitionist **John Brown** stages raid on **Harpers Ferry, VA** in hopes of starting slave revolt. It fails.

1860
1. **Democratic Party** splits. Southern members walk out of the nominating convention to protest Douglas' mollifying "free" states.
2. **Abraham Lincoln** is elected President.
3. **Crittenden Compromise**, to re-establish the principles of the Missouri Compromise, fails.
4. **South Carolina** secedes from the Union.

1861
1. Mississippi, Florida, Alabama, Georgia, Louisiana, and Texas pass secession ordinances and form the **Confederate States of America**, electing **Jefferson Davis** as president.
2. **Kansas** enters the Union as a free state.
3. **Abraham Lincoln** sends a supply ship into **South Carolina** territorial waters to bring food to **Fort Sumter** in Charleston harbor. Given a choice between an attack on the fort or submission, the Carolinians attack.
4. **Civil War/War between the States** has begun.

THE WAR 1861-1865

1861
1. All southern states except **Missouri, Kentucky, Maryland, Delaware, and western Virginia** secede.
2. **Battle of Bull Run**, named for a stream near **Manassas Junction** (Virginia), shows that the war is very real and bloody.
   a. South wins when 9,000 additional troops under **General Thomas Jackson** arrive.
   b. During the battle, a spectator remarked that, amid all the chaos, Jackson is standing *"firm as a stone wall."*
   c. Many Southerners refer to battle as the first Battle of Manassas.
3. **General George McClellan** organizes an expanded Union Army.
4. Union Blockade of southern ports begins.
5. The first **Confiscation Act** is passed allowing seizure of all "property" used for insurrection purposes, including slaves.
6. Detective **Allen Pinkerton** uncovers a plot to assassinate Lincoln, and forms a counterespionage organization that discourages General McClellan from action by exaggerating Confederate troop strength.

1862
1. **Forts Henry** and **Donelson** are captured by Union troops under **U. S. Grant**, opening a major southern route.
2. New Orleans is captured.
3. **Battle of Shiloh**, the bloodiest battle of the war thus far, is fought, altering perceptions of a "short" war.
   a. 13,000 Union dead; 11,000 Confederate dead.
   b. The Union "wins."
4. The Confederacy is forced to adopt a draft.
5. McClellan attacks **Virginia**.
   a. Led by **General Robert E. Lee**, Confederate troops hold off the Union forces.
   b. Buoyed by this, **Jefferson Davis** orders his troops on the offensive.
6. **Second Confiscation Act** orders taking of property of all who support rebellion, even if that "support" is merely living in the south and paying taxes.
7. **Battle of Antietam** leads Lincoln to announce emancipation of all slaves in states whose people *"shall then be in rebellion against the United States"* on January 1, 1863.

1863
1. **National Banking Act** leads to a uniform currency across the nation.
2. The Union adopts a draft.
3. Black soldiers are allowed to join the Union Army. Many remain in service after the war and go west. The Indians call them "Buffalo soldiers," as their dark skin, and tenacity in battle, is like a fierce buffalo.
4. The blockade leads to food riots in many southern cities.
5. **Battle of Chancellorsville** (Virginia) is a surprise victory for the Confederacy over larger Union forces, thanks to the strategy of **Lee** and **Jackson**.
6. **Battle of Gettysburg** (Pennsylvania) is disastrous for the Confederacy, and the turning point in the war. Lee's strategy, which sees over 4,000 dead and 24,000 missing or wounded, is blamed.
7. **Vicksburg** (Mississippi) surrenders.
8. Riots in New York protest the draft.

1864
1. In the Battle of Cold Harbor (Virginia) Grant loses over 12,000 men in just a few hours, but vows to fight it out *"...if it takes all summer."*
2. Lincoln requests a Republican Party platform abolishing slavery nationwide for upcoming election.
3. Union General **William Tecumseh Sherman** enters Atlanta.
4. Lincoln is re-elected.
5. **Jefferson Davis** proposes Confederate emancipation.
6. Sherman's **March to the Sea** in Georgia decimates the countryside. His "scorched earth" policy of burning crops and property leaves nothing in its wake.

1865
1. Sherman continues his drive through the Carolinas.
2. The **Thirteenth Amendment** abolishes slavery.
3. **Hampton Roads Conference** (Virginia) lays the groundwork for southern re-unification into the U.S.
4. **General Robert E. Lee** surrenders to **General Ulysses S. Grant** at the Appomattox Courthouse (Virginia).
5. **John Wilkes Booth** assassinates Lincoln at the performance of *Our American Cousin* at Ford's Theater.
6. **Jefferson Davis is captured**, and remaining Confederate forces lay down their arms.
7. **The war ends.** The Union has lost 360,222 men; the Confederacy 258,000; with over 471,000 wounded on both sides.

RECONSTRUCTION 1865-1877

1865
1. **President Andrew Johnson** starts **Reconstruction**.
2. Confederate leaders rise again.
3. **Black Codes enacted**.
4. Congress refuses seating of Southern Delegates.
5. **Thirteenth Amendment** ratified.

1866 **Fourteenth Amendment** passed, to apply Civil Rights, as guaranteed by The Bill of Rights, to all States. It is rejected by Southern States.

1867
1. **Military Reconstruction Act** is passed.
2. **Tenure of Office Act** is passed.
3. Southern States call Constitutional Convention.
4. Secretary of State **W. H. Seward** purchases **Alaska**.

1868
1. Impeachment/Acquittal of **Andrew Johnson**.
2. Readmission of Southern States.
3. **Fourteenth Amendment** ratified.
4. **Ulysses S. Grant** is elected president.

1870
1. The **Fifteenth Amendment** bars denying voting rights *"on account of race, color, or previous condition of servitude."*
2. First **Enforcement Act**

1871
1. **Ku Klux Klan Act**
2. Second **Enforcement Act**
3. **Treaty of Washington**, designed to settle questions of Canada/U.S. border rights, claims against Britain for damage to the Confederate ship *Alabama*, and some North Atlantic fishing rights, is signed.

1872
1. **Amnesty Act**
2. Debtors want Greenbacks to remain as legal currency.
3. Grant elected to second term.

1873
1. **Slaughterhouse Cases**
2. **Panic of 1873**

1874
1. Grant refuses to increase paper money supply.
2. Democrats become House majority.
3. Congress makes gold sole monetary standard.

1875
1. Corruption indictment of Grant appointees.
2. Passage of new **Civil Rights Act**.
3. Greenbacks to be converted to gold by 1878.

1876
1. *U.S. v Reese*: Constitution *"does not guarantee right to vote."*
2. *U.S. v. Cruikshank*: U.S. has no right to intervene in private discrimination.

1877
1. Congress elects **Rutherford B. Hayes** president after disputes in general election lead many to believe **Samuel Tilden** is winner.
2. African-Amer. "Exodusters" migrate to **Kansas**.

OTHER THINGS... 1857-1877

1857
1. First publication of *Harper's* and *Atlantic Monthly.*
2. New York and St. Louis are connected by rail.

1858
1. **George M. Pullman** puts sleeping cars on trains.
2. *Ladies Christian Assoc.*, later **YWCA**, is formed.

1859
1. The first intercollegiate **baseball** game is played.
2. **Dan D. Emmett**, who has never been to the South, writes *Dixie* for a minstrel show.

1860
1. The **Pony Express** is started and ends, made unnecessary by the telegraph.
2. The first "dime novels" are published.

1861 **Yale** grants the country's first **Ph.D**.

1862 The first enclosed baseball field opens in **Brooklyn**.

1863 Brotherhood of Railway Locomotive Engineers, one of the earliest labor unions, is formed.

1864
1. **"In God we trust"** appears on U.S. coins.
2. Trade Unionism grows with organization of the **Cigar Makers** and **Iron Moulders**.

1865
1. 91 baseball teams in the National Association.
2. **Mark Twain** starts *The Nation.*

1866 Congress authorizes the coining of the nickel.

1868
1. For federal employees, 8-hour workday becomes
2. Amnesty declared for all involved in Civil

1869 First **Intercontinental Railroad** is completed

1870
1. **National Weather Bureau** is established.
2. The first black Senator, **Hiram R. Revels**, is sea

1871 "Greenbacks" (paper money) established as legal te

1872 **Chicago fire** decimates much of the city.

1873 Plagues of grasshoppers devastate western farml

1874 The first bridge to span the Mississippi is open

1875
1. "Osteopathy" developed by **Dr. Andrew T.**
2. **Mary Baker Eddy** publishes *Science and H*

1876 The first **National League baseball** game is pl

1877 George B. Selden makes 2 cylinder "gas carri

CREDITS
Author: Steven M. Berner
Layout: Michael D. Adam

VISIT OUR WEB SITE
www.quickstudycharts.com
or
www.barcharts.com

PRICE
U.S. $ 3.95
CAN $ 5.95

ISBN 157222412-6
9 781572 224124
50395

April 2000
654614 20412 7

NOTE TO STUDENT

This **QUICK STUDY®** chart is an **outline of the basic topics** taught in American History 1 courses. **Keep it handy as a quick reference source in class** and while doing **homework**. Also use it as a **memory refresher** just prior to exams. This chart is an **inexpensive** course supplement designed to **save you time**! Due to its condensed format, use it as a History guide but not as a replacement for assigned class work.